North East Life in the 1930s, 40s & 50s

by Andrew Clark

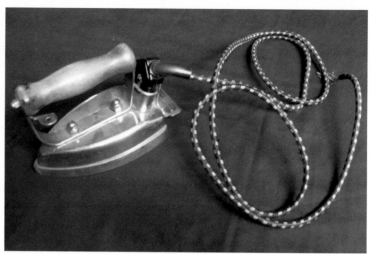

A cobbler's last was found in many homes in the 1930s, 40s and 50s. In those days, worn shoes were repaired as there was not the money to replace them. Shoes and boots would be placed onto the last while a new leather sole was put on or segs were hammered in.

A very basic electric iron from around the 1940s. It is an advance on the old flat irons that were heated on the oven or fire but still hard work. Unlike today's modern irons, this one has no temperature control and so care had to be taken not to burn the clothes. Also it is as heavy or even heavier than a flat iron so must have taken some strength to finish off a day's ironing.

Previous page: Dancing around the May Pole at Dean Bank School, Ferryhill in 1951.

Summerhill Books

Summerhill Books publishes North East local history books.

To receive a catalogue of our titles, send a stamped addressed envelope to:

Andrew Clark, Summerhill Books, PO Box 1210, Newcastle-upon-Tyne NE99 4AH

or email: summerhillbooks@yahoo.co.uk

or visit our website to view our full range of books: **www.summerhillbooks.co.uk**

Copyright Andrew Clark 2015

First published in 2015 by

Summerhill Books
PO Box 1210, Newcastle-upon-Tyne NE99 4AH

www.summerhillbooks.co.uk

email: summerhillbooks@yahoo.co.uk

ISBN: 978-1-906721-96-1

Contents

Domestic science (cookery) class at Newbottle School in May 1952.

Acknowledgements

The author would like to thank the following who have kindly helped with this book:

Alan Brett, John Brett, John Carlson, Harry & Pauline Clark, Jack Curtis, Philip Curtis, Anne Dixon, Jack Hair, Dorothy Hall, Jim Harland, Paul Heslop, Mike Ingoe, Mike Kirkup, George & Phyllis Laws, George Nairn, Colin Orr, Jim Pace, Mary & Neil Taylor, Sharyn Taylor and Hildred Whales.

Beamish Museum – The North of England Open Air Museum
The Chronicle, The Journal, Sunderland Echo
West Newcastle Picture History Collection

Bibliography

Lena Cooper's story 'A Woman's Work is Never Done' was first published in
Women of Old County Durham

Evan Martin's story 'Syrup of Figs and Amami' was first published in
Memories of Bedlington and Beyond

Jack Hair's stories 'Tin Baths and Outside Toilets' and 'The Chocolate Tin were first published in *Looking Back at Stanley*

Colin Orr's story 'Keep The Home Fires Burning' was first published in
Durham Coal – A People's History

Norman Christenson's story 'The Nit Nurse and Empire Day' was first published in
North Shields – Plodgin' Through The Clarts

Paul Heslop's story 'Roy Rogers and the Jungle Girl' was first published in
Westerhope Remembered

Jim Harland's story 'The Roxy Ballroom' was first published in
True Tales of Blyth … and other places

Mary Foster Taylor's story 'Tatie Picking' was first published in
Around The Lyne

Dorothy A. Rand's story 'Christmas Cake and Stocking Fillers' was first published in
Peoples & Places of Old County Durham

Introduction

Although I was born in the 1960s, I am fascinated with life in the 1930s, 40s and 50s. Life in those decades was very different from today but, as those years are within the living memory of many people, it is history that you can easily relate to. I enjoy listening to stories of everyday life at that time and some of those memories are featured in the following pages.

I consider myself lucky in the job I have chosen. I am a local history writer and publisher of over 100 North East books. I also give talks on life before, during and after the Second World War to history societies, community groups, libraries, schools and care homes. I have included in this book my favourite articles from the many publications I have worked on as well as some of the stories told to me at my talks.

The subjects I have chosen to include are the ones I believe people enjoy – such as life at home, entertainment, holidays, Christmas and childhood games. However, this book is just the starting point in our trip down memory lane. If my stories bring back memories you have – please share them. Talk to your friends and family about your life and pass on to them the unique history we have in the North East.

Andrew Clark
Summerhill Books, 2015

A hearth and kitchen range in a North East home. To the right is a hand wash tub and mangle.

Some of the objects I use in my talks, on the stage at South Shields Library. Left to right: two poss sticks, washboard, poss tub, tongs and tin bath.

When Monday Was Always Wash Day

Who remembers when Monday was always wash day? And who remembers when the washing was always done in a poss tub with a poss stick and mangle? Two types of poss sticks are on the right – a wooden one and a metal version.

There was plenty of hard work in the shipyards, pits and factories but there was also plenty of hard work at home for the mams who didn't have all the modern gadgets we take for granted today. So most housewives had what they called the weekly agenda with a job for each day, that would probably take all day to complete. And Monday was always wash day. All day was spent washing, with the clothes pegged out on the line in the back lane.

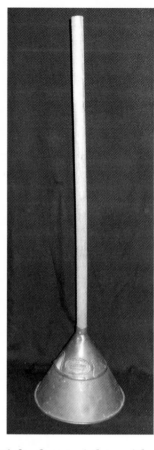

The poss stick above right, with a copper base, is called 'The Swiftsure'. Made by the British Vacuum Washing Company, when pushed down a vacuum is created that sucks up water to help with the possing.

Left: Gertie Dawson on wash day in the backyard of her house at New Lambton, County Durham, in the 1930s. She is using a wooden poss stick and tub with a mangle fitted. Can you imagine young mams today using a poss tub? All you do now is put your clothes in a machine, press a button and then walk away – easy! Remember coming home on washing day when it was raining? There would be steaming clothes everywhere. And for tea on Monday it was always leftovers from the Sunday dinner.

In some colliery communities, wash day was known as 'The Devil's Birthday' as it was such hard work.

Another piece of equipment from washing day – the mangle used to squeeze out the water from the clothes before putting them on the line.

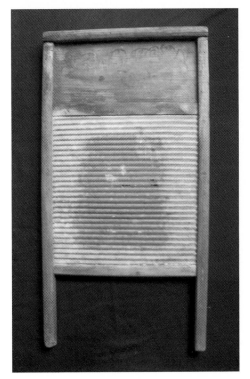

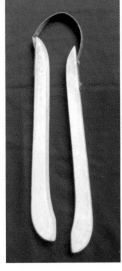

Above: Washing became easier when the twin tub was introduced. Here is Bruce Forsyth advertising a twin tub for 52 guineas or £11 12s deposit and 10s 2d weekly for two years. At this price, no wonder some housewives continued to use their poss tub well into the 1960s.

Left: Tongs – essential for lifting the clothes out of the hot water.

Left: As well as poss sticks and tubs, some mams used a washboard. They also had another use as a musical instrument in skiffle bands. The most famous skiffle musician was Lonnie Donegan whose song 'Rock Island Line' featured a washboard.

A Woman's Work is Never Done

by Lena Cooper

In the 1930s the variety of jobs open to women where I lived was somewhat limited. There was the local brick factory (Lumley Brickworks) which employed women to deal with some of the brick-making processes. In 1935/36 I was told of a vacancy in the office of the Chester-le-Street Co-operative Society Bakery Department. Being advised to apply for the post, I did and got the job. At the time I had no idea what was involved in this. I discovered that my starting time was 6 am and the finishing time could be around 3 or 4 pm.

On my first morning, I had to be out of bed at 5 am, dressed, breakfasted and on my way for my three mile walk to Chester-le-Street to start work at 6 am. At that time there were no service buses before 6 am.

When I got to work, my first job was in the office, checking the bakery orders from the various Co-op Branches and taking orders by telephone. When all the orders were written up they were taken into the bakehouse for their attention and packing on to the bakery boards for the vans to do branch deliveries.

My next duty was to stay in the bakehouse and grease tins for that day's batch of pies, cakes etc. The bakehouse was on the first floor and below at the ground level was the tea-room. On odd occasions I was told to service the tea-room. That was where I learned how to make a pot of tea and how to toast a teacake.

Lena Cooper.

After a while I was able to get transferred to the Fencehouses Branch in the drapery department. The bakery was to be closed. Nothing to do with me – honest!

So it was much better in all ways – start at 9 am and just a short walk to work. I was about 17 years old and reckoned I only had to put in one year in this job then I could apply to become a nurse, which was what I wanted to be – but I had to be 18 before I could apply.

Working in the drapery department of the Fencehouses Branch was enjoyable up to a point but I hated having to do the chores at home that involved getting my nails dirty!

Lena worked in the Fence Houses branch of the Chester-le-Street Co-operative Society and here is the grocery department in the 1930s.

The worst job – in those pre-war days – was cleaning the 'pit-clothes'. These were worn by male members of the family who worked down the local pit. Each item of clothing was full of coaldust and had to be 'dadded' against the wall in the back street to get rid of this. Then with an old knife the pit boots had to be freed from all the 'clarts' and rubbish that had built up on the sides and bottom of the boots, then greased.

I never understood why it was always my job to do this, just as it was always my job to scrub the scullery (kitchen) and pantry floors on a washing day after I got home from my job at the Co-op drapery department.

Invariably Monday was the day for washing for the whole family. I once tried my hand at 'possing' but it was not easy to lift the 'poss stick' let alone hit the clothes with any downward pressure. Tuesdays and Wednesdays were for ironing and putting clean clothes away, then the bedrooms had to be cleaned. Thursday was baking day – with pies, teacakes, bread, scones, sponge cakes, custard tarts, and sometimes jam tarts and small queen cakes. All day was used for baking the food for the family to last for about a week.

Friday was always cleaning downstairs of the house from front door to backyard and occasionally after lunch there was some shopping to be done.

Saturdays were sometimes used for shopping according to how much spare cash was available for items required. This did not happen every week – just once in a while.

The Sabbath Day was kept holy. I went to the local chapel in the morning. We went to Sunday school after dinner, then back to chapel again in the evening. And we always wore our 'Sunday Best' clothes.

Most mams had a day for baking. *Above:* A bread bin that has been well used over the years. The word 'bread' has faded from the side. *Left:* A Be-Ro Home Recipes book for scones, cakes, pastry and puddings.

A carpet beater used to 'dad' the mats.

A lady cleans her windows in Boathouse Terrace, Cambois, Northumberland on 'outside day'. Other jobs on outside day included: donkey stoning the steps and cleaning the backyard.

Ironing Day

There was plenty of hard work to be done on a Monday wash day but it wasn't easy on a Tuesday either – ironing day. For many this meant a heavy flat iron (*right*) heated on the kitchen range. And how did you know it was hot enough? Yes, you spat on it!

A cloth around the handle would provide some protection from the heat but this was a hard day's work with clothes, sheets and other items all being ironed.

Some irons had a large base that a metal block fitted inside. This block, known as a pig, was heated up instead of the whole iron and this extra weight must have made it even heavier. Other irons were heated by gas and I've been told plenty of stories of how dangerous they were with flames shooting out of the back!

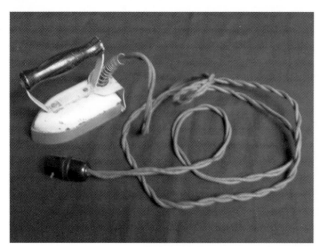

Left is an early electric iron. It's quite small and looks like a travel iron. I've spoken to some ladies who worked in laundries and they said they used something similar when ironing delicates. Note the plug is one that would go into the socket on a light. Some light fittings had two sockets, one for the bulb and another for electric items. Dave Best of Swalwell History Society told me that his mam used an electric iron plugged into the light. When she ironed the light would be swinging from side to side. This caused his dad some problems while reading his newspaper so he would be constantly moving his paper to catch the light from the swinging bulb.

Right: Girls in a North East school learning how to use flat irons and scrubbing boards. This photograph is from the early 1900s but I have spoken to many women who, even in the 1950s, were taught basic washing and ironing skills like this at school – using flat irons, poss sticks and washboards.

Syrup of Figs and Amami

by Evan Martin

Friday was a day many of us young 'uns faced with apprehension in the colliery villages around Bedlington. With school finished for two days and a weekend to enjoy, many mothers took advantage of no school to dose us with Syrup of Figs. The expression 'Yiv nivvor been moved for a couple o' days. Ye need a gud physickin', was undoubtedly heard in many houses on a Friday night. The fact that Friday was known as bath, bash & physic night was not surprising. None of us had bathrooms and hot water from the set pot poured into the tin bath with a metal ewer, was the bath part. The bash was often what mother gave after a chase around the table with a spoonful of this dire tasting fluid in her hand. It always went down, followed by a Horlicks tablet and the announcement from Dad, that in his day it was castor oil on a Friday night, which apparently was worse than Syrup of Figs and was supposed to make me feel better. Granda, when he was there, proved how hard his generation was when he went one better by letting us all know his mother gave him and his brothers raw paraffin oil. This, apparently, was poured into an open mouth while he pinched his nostrils. 'It wis elwis teckin at sivin o'clock and wis doon through wi by haff past ten.'

I forever thought how lucky it was Granda didn't smoke. He would probably have gone up in flames.

Not anywhere near as bad as Syrup of Figs was mother's own concoction to clean the skin and clear the passages: Salts & Lemon. Lemons were cut up and mixed with Epsom Salts; boiling water poured over, jugged, covered, left to settle and then forced down your neck any night or morning, not just Friday.

Evan Martin in his pram.

Above and right: some of the remedies that Evan Martin remembers that were used mother to cure all ills – Zam-Buk herbal balm, Beecham's Pills and Camphorated Oil.

I didn't have a sister but my cousin Norah, Aunt Lil's eldest daughter, was as near as makes no difference. She was a lot older than me but she often stayed weekends and she and her friend Vida Tait called Friday night 'Amami Night'.

Amami was apparently a shampoo which could make your hair like Rita Hayworth's and Margaret Lockwood's. I remember as an eight year old sending Norah's picture to Rita Hayworth in Hollywood, telling her that our Norah used Amami shampoo and asked if she liked it too. A few weeks later I got an envelope, USA stamped and franked in Los Angeles, with a picture of Rita Hayworth and signed by her. She never mentioned whether or not she was an 'Amami' night girl too.

Rita Hayworth.

Tin Baths and Outside Toilets

by Jack Hair

Hanging on a hook in our back yard at Delacour Street in Stanley was our tin bath. At that time we had no hot water systems or bathroom. The water had to be heated either in the boiler at the side of the coal fire or in pans on the gas cooker.

On bath nights, Mam would heat up loads of water and bring in the galvanised tin bath from the yard. The bath was placed on the mat in front of the fire and the hot water was added. We would take it in turns to have a bath with Mam changing the water as often as was needed.

This bath was oval in shape with handles on each end. You had to step into and out of the bath very carefully in case you spilt it. Even though this may sound strange, it was an enjoyable experience to bathe with the lights out, with only the light from the flames of the coal fire illuminating the room, giving you some small amount of privacy.

We used to use the long bars of soap such as Fairy or Sunlight bought at the Co-op of course. Sometimes I can still feel the raised embossed ridges of the bottom of this bath in my backside today.

Jack Hair, aged 12.

Here is an oval-shaped tin bath, as described by Jack Hair, and a young boy ready for a wash with soap and towel. Or is he? If you look closely, behind the lad is a painted backdrop and so this picture was probably taken in a photographer's studio. Although this isn't a true representation of 'bath night', it is still a lovely photograph.

One memory of those childhood days in Delacour Street still brings a smile to my face. In our double tenement house there were five of us living downstairs and a family of seven upstairs. There was only one outside toilet for all of us and this was a water closet type toilet.

One winter, when the toilet pipes were frozen making it unusable, Mrs Watson, a family friend, allowed us to use her ash midden type toilet, known locally as the netty. This brick building was out in the yard with the outside wall facing the back street. Inside was a wooden box type toilet. In the top of this box was a round hole covered with a wooden lid. You would lift the lid and sit on the hole just like sitting on a normal toilet. The principle of an ash midden toilet was that ashes from the fire were tipped into the hole thus covering the toilet deposits, for want of a better explanation.

Few of these toilets had the luxury of toilet paper and the norm was for a newspaper to be cut into squares and placed on a nail on the wall. This was the place that most people learned of the news of the day. It was quite dark in the toilet due to there being only a very small darkened window in the door. The only other light came in by way of an air brick for ventilation.

One day, when I was using this toilet, I was sitting there reading, and all of a sudden there was a great rush of air up my backside. I jumped up off the seat and turned around with my trousers dangling around my ankles. Before me I saw what can only be described as a beam of light shining upward out of the hole in the seat like a ray from heaven. Flying around in this beam of light were small flies. I peered down into the ash midden and there before me was a great long-handled shovel cleaning out the waste from the midden.

It was of course the council refuse man. They came around once a week to remove the waste from the ash middens. What an awful job, and what a fright.

Right: A scavenger cart in Shiney Row, around 1930. At the back of the cart you can see the long-handled shovels used to empty the netties.

Left: Towneley Street in Stanley with a row of outside toilets on the far left – across the back lane from people's homes.

Below: The back lane of Railway Terrace, Wallsend, in 2014. The former hatches of the coalhouses are half way down the wall. At the bottom of the wall can just be seen the bricked-up old doors that were opened to allow the cleaning of the outside toilets. The men doing this work were often called 'midnight mechanics'.

Keep The Home Fires Burning

by Colin Orr

If your dad worked at the pit, and most did, then you were all right for coals. A warm living room was guaranteed, even if bedrooms on biting winter nights were as cold as Greenland's icy mountains.

Our council house in The Crescent, Silksworth was different from the colliery cottages that had been designed with a constant, plentiful supply of coal in mind. This struck me on visits to Uncle Andy and Aunt Jennie and to a fireplace behind which it appeared possible to throw half a ton of coals. There, when the fire needed building up, a trip to the coalhouse was not needed. Only an arm's length away on the hearth lay the coal rake and a few forward strokes of this had the flames shooting up the chimney in seconds. Further replenishments could be made without exhausting what lay there. I'm certain when I say that loads were delivered at not less than three, but not more than four, weekly intervals – something like 25 days to be more precise. The ticket had to be put in, as the saying went, and within a few days the coal motor was heading in your direction. It would be bad management if your coalhouse was empty and you were borrowing to keep a fire going before the coals were dumped. Occasionally, though, and particularly during a hard winter, the bottom of the coalhouse might be only inches away from view. By then, for certain, you would be burning what was known as duff. This was not much more than coal dust, a shovelful of which had a dramatic beneficial effect, but only momentarily. It quickly caked the surface and deadened the glow.

Colin Orr.

The newly-supplied load almost surely contained a lot of roundies (large chunks of coal) and the transformation by burning this was both pleasing and cheering. The fire had a fresh vitality and a sense of contentment settled on the household. The day was made and it didn't seem a bad thing after all to have a dad who worked at the pit, dirty and dangerous though the job was. Reading your Biggles book, or listening to Radio Stagshaw or Radio Droitwich, had an enjoyable added dimension. With the flames licking into those roundies, a retreat was required. To stay too close quickly gave you what was popularly referred to as corned-beef legs, a condition that more readily affected the ladies.

Should a neighbour, or someone in the Co-op butcher queue, announce that, 'It's rubbish they are leaving at present,' then here was bad news for those expecting a delivery. Rubbish signified coal of inferior quality, perhaps with as much duff as roundies and, more importantly, a big share of stones. Such loads reflected the nature of the coal currently being mined and little could be done. They had not to be interpreted as a spiteful act by the management should output have fallen away. Stones were easily identified, a lighter colour to start with, heavier too, and the large pieces set aside. Small fragments, however, could make their way on to the fire with noisy and potentially dangerous consequences. Now, the back-away exercise was not due to excessive heat, but in a bid to find shelter.

That Bobby Thompson joke about China figures, notably one of Napoleon, in a miner's cottage lifting their arms to protect themselves from flying pieces of hot stone had everything to do with such a load of coal. It would need no explanation in mining communities.

HOW ARE YOU OFF FOR COALS?

An advert for coal when this fuel was used in almost every home.

Two smiling ladies from Ashington hoyin' in the coals.

It was often a job for young 'uns to put away the coal after a delivery.

Once a pit mishap had reduced the number of my dad's legs from two to one, to make him a compensation case, the job of housing our coals fell to brother Albert, and me. If that brightly-burning fire initiated by a new delivery was the plus, then getting it into the coalhouse was a minus.

Washing day was known as the Devil's Birthday, but this was Old Nick's Christmas Day. To count each shovelful that our juvenile limbs hurled through the hatch was the worst thing to do. Complete demoralisation set in when, on reaching 50, the load looked no smaller. Hours and many aching bones later, just enough energy remained to climb into the bath and then into bed. The thought did not strike me then, but it does now, that coals and me did not mix. Thank goodness, I would be leaving school when the opportunities were such that you had not to follow your dad into the pit.

Mine did, and thousands others too. No fun. Hard work if putting in a load of coals was anything to go by.

Right: Two pitmen in a Northumberland Colliery working in cramped underground conditions.

The Happiest Days of Your Life

by Norman Christenson

Wor Ma was forever telling us to enjoy our schooldays because they'd be the happiest days of our entire lives. Many's the time I dragged my weary feet up to the High School, the rain dripping off my nose end as I tried to work out whether I'd be in more trouble for being late, or for the undone algebra homework that was due that morning, or for the history book that I'd lost somewhere or other. And the thought often crossed my mind that if these were the happiest days of my life then I must have a hell of a lot of pain and misery ahead of me. But it wasn't always like that.

I couldn't wait to start school and I can see myself dragging Wor Ma along West Percy Road at a gallop as we marched off for my very first day at Queen Victoria Junior School. QV, all solid and square and respectable, two and a bit floors of red brick relieved only by the odd yellow blocks inset above and alongside some of the tall windows that the teachers opened and closed with great long poled hooks that may well have been used at the Battle of Agincourt.

Norman Christenson.

We boys seldom got above the ground floor, the higher floors seemingly reserved for stuff like domestic science, a none too scientific subject, where the girls learned to bathe stiff porcelain dolls in tin tubs and cook exotic meals like toad in the hole and cottage pie. Sister Doreen went there later and she used to bring home stuff for the rest of us to try, but despite Wor Ma's very best warning looks and threatening headshakes, it invariably ended in tears as we three lads choked and spat and rolled on the floor clutching our throats in a manner that was clearly not intended to show our intense appreciation of her culinary efforts.

I loved QV even though you'd never guess it from the sole picture I have of our class taken when I was seven or eight years old, twenty four of us, exactly fifty-fifty boys and girls all staring suspiciously at the strange man with the big camera and the flash thing that went off with a better bang than most of the fireworks we got for Guy Fawkes' Night.

Norman's only class photograph from Queen Victoria School, North Shields, around 1939. He is third left in the front row.

Schooling in the 1930s was light years away from today's liberated methods. It operated on some fairly simple and basic criteria, the most important of which was that we knew absolutely nothing, the teachers knew absolutely everything so if we shut up and sat there and listened for long enough there was just an outside possibility that we might learn something. Our first few years were spent 'doing our letters' on small slates and endlessly reciting our times tables in classrooms where our piping young voices bounced off the high ceilings and walls that were adorned only by the bare necessities, namely a picture of HM the King and a map of the world that rolled up into a long metal tube. No matter what time of day you passed that school you'd have heard one or more classes intoning their 'three times three is nine, four times three is twelve, five times ...' like so many Gregorian monks working their way through some ancient catechism.

It's easy to sneer at these primitive methods today when six-year-olds can sit at a computer and calculate the square root of 632 quicker than we could sharpen our pencils but it's worth remembering that this generation would one day work in shops and factories where they'd be expected to calculate the price of six ounces of best butter at one and fourpence ha'penny a pound or seven feet of fabric at seven and six a yard. Not only would they carry out these calculations while the customer stood over them purse in hand, but they'd do them with nothing more than the ubiquitous stub of pencil on the corner of the paper in which the butter or cloth or whatever was wrapped. And more often than not they'd get it right!

A boys' exercise class at Queen Victoria School, North Shields, in the 1930s.

The Nit Nurse

Our daily routine was broken two or three times a year when the district nurse bowled into the class with her surgical tray, her tooth comb and her steely-eyed determination to stamp out the head lice (dickies). Sat at the raised teacher's table, she'd glare disapprovingly at us as we all struggled to get to the back of the queue that our teacher pushed and prodded us into. The routine that followed was well established. As each kid stepped forward, nursey grasped them firmly by the upper arm with a grip that usually left five red finger prints if you stood still and five black and blue ones if you didn't. The official small toothcomb was dipped into the prussic acid or whatever it was she used to sanitise it then dragged through your hair four or five times. All my life, I always wanted to have lovely curly hair, all my life, that is, except this one day when our shaved cut was a decided advantage. Not so, the poor girls and the curly tops who stood silently, teeth clenched, eyes welling as the comb snagged and pulled and tugged before finally tearing clear, its teeth clenched around handfuls of golden tresses. The offending locks were inspected minutely by the nurse. Satisfied that the comb and entangled locks were free from vermin, the victim was then waved disdainfully back to his or her seat where we all sat with burning scalps, glad to be through the ordeal and even gladder to be spared the ignominy of being handed the little slip of paper which nursey filled in with great relish for those poor kids who suffered the embarrassment of being found to be infected. I often thought afterwards that it would have been more appropriate if she'd donned a black cap whenever she filled in the dreaded dickey docket.

Empire Day

The tedium of times tables, letters and spelling bees was broken yet again for a far more eagerly anticipated occasion, when the junior school put on its special annual extravaganza to celebrate Empire Day. Come the great day, we picked fresh daisies that Wor Ma, and countless others, carefully wrapped in cigarette foil before pinning them to coats or jumpers. Then off we marched with the more excitable of us singing:

'Twenty fourth of May, the Queen's birthday ... If we don't get a holiday we'll all run away'

as we each tried to remember the parts we'd play in the events we'd been rehearsing for weeks previously. One year we did this fantastic gymnastic display where kids dived through hoops, walked along upside down wooden forms, skipped through ropes and, in a staggering grand finale ran at a strip of matting where we 'cowped wor kreels' not once but twice before standing all red faced and dizzy to take our well-deserved plaudits.

As great a spectacle as this undoubtedly was, it would be put well and truly in the shade the next year when I was to play a starring role in our epic tribute to the Empire. By mid-morning, the playground was a sea of faces as proud parents and grandparents were shepherded behind carefully chalked lines by bossy teachers while even bossier teachers, inside the school, prepared the cast of thousands (well at least a hundred or so anyway) for the imminent De Millian showcase. Finally everything was in place. While 'God Save The King' was played on our battered old piano, four kids carefully raised the Union Jack to the top of the flagpole where it flapped proudly over the headmaster as he welcomed honoured guests and parents and declared the festivities duly opened. Now it was my turn. Swallowing nervously I marched smartly to the centre of the playground and onto the elaborate dais made from two milk crates wrapped in red, white and blue paper. A tense hush settled over the crowd as I carefully unrolled the ornate scroll off one of the two twelve inch rulers and in my poshest of posh voices started to introduce the great and colourful cavalcade. 'Welcome to our brave and noble savages from sunny, far off Tanganyika' at which a group of

North Shields children pose for Empire Day.

beaming kids marched proudly out, all wrapped in stripy cloth, their faces glowing beneath the cocoa make-up. They were followed by 'Our fearsome Gurkha friends from afar who stood by our side in the Great War' again clad in the same striped cloth but this time waving cardboard knives in their hands. Then, 'Our proud lumberjack friends from the frozen wastes of far off Canada' this time followed by a gaggle of smug white-faced kids carrying make believe axes and dressed in tartan winter jackets and astrakhan hats. This had been one of the harder groups to outfit as most of us kids didn't have a jacket of any description let alone one of those tartan ones that any of us would have killed for. The girls and the striped cloth and cocoa got back into the act as 'We warmed our wintry British days with tea from far off Ceylon'. And so it went on till the last of the mostly brown-faced and stripy-clothed kids had marched past the dais and come to a halt facing the audience who nudged neighbours as they pointed out their very own offspring. Then a teacher struck up 'Land of Hope and Glory', we all sang as if our lungs would burst, the teachers stood proud and proprietorial, the mothers and grandmothers looked at each other and snuffled and the odd dad sniffed and pretended he had something in his eye. The headmaster declared proceedings closed, we kids cheered and ran to receive the admiration of our parents and to walk home together for the half-day holiday. It was days like this that made you proud to be British and best.

The Chocolate Tin

by Jack Hair

During the Second World War, and for several years after, there was still a great shortage of many of the goods in the shops, such as fresh fruit, sweets, etc. Around 1946/47 I went to Stanley Board School and, on occasions, food parcels were sent to the area from places such as Russia and Canada. The Russian miners sent parcels in metal containers and had in them such things as dried egg powder and small round biscuits which were so hard they had to be soaked before you could eat them, boiled fruit sweets and hard, dark chocolate.

The Canadians often sent crates full of large red juicy apples. These were distributed to the children in schools. Occasionally, the teachers would give out Horlicks tablets which were small, hard, oblong sweets wrapped in paper which tasted revolting.

A queue in the hall meant one of two things. Either you were going to be given something to eat or it was the Nit Nurse. One day the teacher told us all to bring into school a tin or jar with a lid for the next day. We realised at once that we were going to be given something so I took into school a large, dried baby milk food tin. At the end of the day we were given our tins and to our surprise they were filled to the top with sweetened chocolate powder.

We tasted it and were well pleased and spent most of that night licking the chocolate powder off our sticky little fingers. Next day the teacher informed us there was still powder left and to bring our tins in again. We hunted until we found the biggest tins we could and once again they filled them. I might tell you we ate chocolate powder for days until our jaws ached and our fingers were thin and pale with continuously sucking them. As an adult I now know we must have appeared greedy but at that time with no sweets, no money and food shortages it was like leaving an alcoholic in a brewery.

Right: A ration book from 1953-54, the last year of rationing. A lot of people held onto the last ration book – perhaps they thought it would come back. Food rationing started at the beginning of the Second World War and continued for nine years after the war had ended.

Far right: The points page for sweets from a ration book.

A gentleman in Wallsend told me his ration allowed him to get a chocolate bar and a packet of gums. He would cut the bar into seven pieces and each day he would have one little bit of chocolate. He also divided the gums up in the same way.

Going Bananas

It is said that during the time of rationing, if you saw a queue … you joined it! I was speaking to a ladies group in Easington and everyone of them could remember when bananas first came back into the shops after the war. They said the queue was up the street but, when you got to the front, all you were allowed was one banana. Then when I was in Benwell in Newcastle, a lady said the same thing happened when this precious fruit was in the shops where she lived. But she queued up just to look at one as she had never seen one before. A gentleman in South Shields went one better. He told me a lad in his class had a banana which he'd eaten at home. When the teacher found out, he had to bring in the skin for the whole class to have a sniff of it.

Radio Times

For many years the main form of entertainment at home wasn't the television it was the radio – or should I say the wireless.

What radio programmes do you remember? Normally when I ask that question, the first two answers are 'Dick Barton – Special Agent' and 'ITMA' with Tommy Handley.

Children would run into the house from playing in the street to listen to daily episodes of Dick Barton with that famous theme tune ('The Devil's Gallop' by Charles Williams). The programme always ended with a cliff hanger with our hero or his friend, Snowy White, in some form of danger. So you had to make sure you heard the following day's episode.

The comedy 'ITMA' – It's That Man Again – is also fondly remembered with its many catchphrases. The show made its star, Tommy Handley, a household name. Sadly, Handley died of a stroke in 1949 and the show ended as it was thought no other comedian could replace him.

Tommy Handley.

Valentine Dyall – best known for his radio series character 'The Man in Black'. He was also a regular on TV and, in his later years, appeared in Doctor Who and Blackadder.

Another radio show that was hard to forget was 'Appointment with Fear' with Valentine Dyall – 'The Man in Black'. I've spoken to people who were terrified by his stories of mystery and horror. His most famous story was the 'Beast with Five Fingers', the tale of a man who was murdered but his severed hand lived on after his death. This hand sought revenge on the people who had killed him and you could hear it scuttling around the room – most likely giving you shivers down you spine. Valentine Dyall would always start with: 'This is your storyteller, the man in black …'

Music programmes have always been popular and, in the 1940s and 50s, millions of people would tune in to programmes such as: 'Friday Night is Music Night', 'Billy Cotton's Bandshow', 'Family Favourites', 'Workers' Playtime', 'Music While You Work' and 'Pick of the Pops'.

Other shows that were popular included: 'In Town Tonight', 'Journey into Space', 'The Navy Lark', 'Listen with Mother', 'Mrs Dale's Diary', 'The Goon Show' and 'Hancock's Half Hour' as well as 'The Archers' and 'Woman's Hour' which are still going strong today.

An advert for the 'Airmaster Eight' for 16 guineas from 1940.

Accumulators

Many of the old wireless sets were powered by accumulators which were large glass batteries filled with acid. They had to be regularly charged up at a local garage, hardware store or cycle shop. You normally had two with one in use and the other on charge. It was often the job of a young 'un to take these acid-filled accumulators off to be charged up.

A110 "Connoisseur"— Designed for faultless listening on 4 stations of your own choice. No tuning scale, single switch tuning. Also ideal for record reproduction. A.C. mains.

18 gns. *tax paid*

An advert for a 'Connoisseur' wireless set from 1950.

Left: My own personal favourite radio programme is 'Educating Archie' with Peter Brough – the ventriloquist on the radio! The show was very popular and many future stars appeared alongside 'Archie', the dummy, including: Julie Andrews, Bruce Forsyth, Dick Emery and Benny Hill. It is said that Peter Brough was a poor ventriloquist and when he appeared on television you could see his lips move – so radio was ideal for him!

Right: An advert for 'Stars of Radio Times' who were appearing at Newcastle's Theatre Royal in 1950. Top of the Bill was Max Wall from 'Variety Band-Box' a show for comedians and the top big bands of the day. Beryl Reid became a successful television and film actress but started her career playing 'Monica' on 'Educating Archie'. The Hedley Ward Trio were another act who had appeared with Peter Brough and Archie Andrews.

RONDAY PRODUCTIONS LTD. present
STARS OF
★ RADIO TIMES ★
A MUSICAL COCKTAIL WITH A GREAT CAST INCLUDING
The Famous Comedian MAX WALL From "Variety Band-Box"
DICK JAMES • BERYL REID • THE HEDLEY WARD TRIO
Singing Star   Radio's "Monica"   From "Educating Archie"

Dick James was a singer with bands such as Henry Hall and Geraldo. He later went into music publishing and made a fortune when he was asked by the Brian Epstein, the manager of the Beatles, to set up a company to control the rights of the group's songs.

The Coronation edition of the Radio Times in 1953.

Ovaltineys

While I was giving a talk at a care home in Lambton, I was asking the residents what radio programmes they remember. Lena Cooper, who was 90 years old, mentioned that her favourite show was the Ovaltineys that was broadcast on Radio Luxembourg. She then sang the words of the famous song:

We are the Ovaltineys,
Little girls and boys;
Make your requests, we'll not refuse you,
We are here just to amuse you.
Would you like a song or story,
Will you share our joys?
At games and sports we're more than keen;
No merrier children could be seen,
Because we all drink Ovaltine,
We're happy girls and boys!

When she had finished she got a round of applause from all of the residents of the home.

Early Television

Right: An advert for televisions from 1953. A 'Pye' 14 inch model cost £64 18 shillings while a 'Ecko' table 12 inch model was £64.

Today almost every home must have a television and these are often hi-tech, colour with large screens. However, can you remember the size of your first TV set? Perhaps with a screen of only 10 or 12 inches and of course it would be in black and white. And what was the first programme you watched? It was probably the Queen's Coronation in 1953 but you would be lucky if one person in your family or even one house in your street had a television. So everyone would crowd into the homes with a set, with the bairns on the floor, all the seats filled and people standing at the back all watching a tiny screen with poor reception.

Do you remember how long it would take to warm up before you could start watching it? And no remote controls in those days – you had to get out of your seat to change the channel.

Below: A crowd of people watching the Coronation on a television in the window of the Rediffusion store in Bedlington. Most of them are wrapped up as even though it was June, it was a cold, wet day.

All of these early televisions were black and white and colour was not introduced until the late 1960s. I have spoken to a few people who remember a piece of film that was placed over the screen to give the effect of watching in colour. It was blue at the top, green at the bottom and an amber colour in the middle. So it was fine if you were watching a programme like 'The Adventures of Robin Hood' with Richard Greene where you had blue for the sky, green for grass and amber for Robin and his Merry Men. But if you were watching someone read the news then their head would be blue, they had an amber body and their desk would be green!

A more common 'gadget' to improve your viewing was the magnifying glass some people had to make these small screens look bigger.

Apart from the Coronation, the most remembered early television programme was Quatermass. Many recall sitting terrified watching this early science fiction show and it was said that it was the first programme ever shown that people rushed home to see and then talked about the next day. There were three series starting with the 'Quatermass Experiment' in 1953 then 'Quatermass II' in 1955 and finally, and most famously, 'Quatermass and the Pit' three years later. All three series were remade for the cinema by Hammer Films.

An illustration showing a 'cabinet' style television set with doors.

The poster of the film version of the 'Quatermass Xperiment'. An 'X' was used in the title to exploit the film ratings of that time which gave horror films an 'X' rating. This version was released in cinemas two years after the original television programme had been broadcast.

One of the stars of the 'Quatermass Xperiment' was Jack Warner who was a very popular film and television actor in the 1940s and 50s. His most famous role was 'Dixon of Dock Green' (left).

Other early shows included 'Dixon of Dock Green' that was broadcast from 1955 to 1976; 'Panorama' that started in 1953; 'Emergency – Ward 10' that ran for ten years from 1957; and 'The Grove Family', thought to be the first soap opera and was shown from 1954 to 1957.

An advert from 1955 encouraging people to buy a television to watch Newcastle in the FA Cup Final.

Coronation Day

Right: Children from Greenside, near Ryton, dressed up for the Coronation of Queen Elizabeth II in June 1953. On the 'Ye Old Coronation Coach' is 'Queen' Norma Cairns. The day was organised by the local butcher, Thomas Eddy, who is dressed in the top hat. There were celebrations like this in every community in the North East.

Left: The front page of the 'Newcastle Journal' on Coronation Day, 2nd June 1953. It shows the dress the Queen was to wear but the headline is about the other major news event that day – Everest was climbed for the first time.

Left: Many people received Coronation mugs or other souvenirs.

Right: Queen Salote of Tonga was one of the guests at the Coronation. The weather was terrible that day but she, unlike the other guests, insisted on having an open carriage for the journey to Westminster Abbey. She is remembered for smiling and waving at the crowds from her carriage

The Silver Screen

Today, going to the pictures is a first class experience with good seats, the most up-to-date equipment and plentiful refreshments. However, for many years a lot of cinemas were known as flea pits or lop houses. At some cinemas you could gain free entry by handing over a jam jar – an early form of recycling that was common before the Second World War but did continue in some areas until the 1950s.

Before television became established in the late 1950s, going to the pictures was one of the favourite forms of entertainment. It would be common to go two or three times a week with most communities having several local cinemas. You could also travel to one of the bigger picture houses who may be showing the latest films. As well as the 'main feature', there would be a 'B' movie, a newsreel, cartoon and trailers.

These were also the days when the beam of light from the projector would cut through a thick cloud of smoke from everyone's cigarettes.

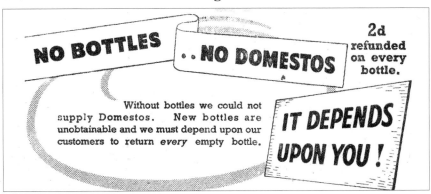

An advert for recycling from after the Second World War. This advert is for Domestos bleach bottles that earned 2d for every returned bottle. One lady told me that the Regal cinema in Monkseaton would allow you free entry for two weeks if you took in an old bleach bottle.

Not all cinemas were flea pits and here is the art-deco interior of the luxurious Savoy in South Shields which was opened in 1936. Films released that year included: Charlie Chaplin's 'Modern Times', 'Swing Time' with Fred Astair and Ginger Rogers, 'The Charge of the Light Brigade' starring Errol Flynn and the very popular 'Flash Gordon' serial.

Roy Rogers and the Jungle Girl

by Paul Heslop

Westerhope Picture Hall was built in 1912 by Sam Piper and his sons, who were all miners at North Walbottle Colliery. It was indeed a palace as it was brick built and most of the others in the district were wooden structures. It was called 'The Orion', but sometimes we called it 'Old Sam's' after the name of its owner. Mainly, though, it was 'the flicks' or 'the pictures', and, cruelly, 'the flea pit'. Whatever its name, it was our local cinema.

When we were young, the cinema was an important part of our lives. No-one had TV then, except, that is, the local Co-op, where we peered through the shop window at the flickering black and white picture on our way home from school. Sometimes we'd sneak into the shop for a closer look. Then we'd be able to listen, too, but such a privilege could last a few minutes only, for discovery would result in being ordered out.

My first memories of the Orion were as a young boy. I went with my parents, mainly. Dad liked westerns; Mum's favourites were what were loosely described as 'love stories'.

When very young, I could not understand why cars on the screen drove on the opposite side of the road. Later, I could identify spelling mistakes in words such as 'Technicolor'. I was, of course, viewing American films.

Pupils from Westerhope Council School outside the Orion during the Second World War.

Most communities had their own cinema in those days not too close, not too far away. This meant competition for the Orion, but so many films were on in the course of just one week at each cinema, you could stick to one and still enjoy a varied selection.

There was a main feature on Monday and Tuesday, another on Wednesday and Thursday and another again on Friday and Saturday. There was yet another on Sunday.

Each was preceded by a 'B' movie. Along with trailers (anything with Randolph Scott was a must) and advertisements, there would sometimes be Pathe News. Alternatively, Coal News would be shown, the latter a sort of propaganda production aimed (one supposes) at the locals, many of whom including my father were coal miners. Looking back, I wonder how he felt, watching miners drilling the coal face to the sound of music?

Such was the popularity of the cinema, it was not uncommon for Old Sam's to be so packed that people stood in the aisles. There would be no complaints about this, not from folk who were only too pleased to have got in. As I recall, the Orion bulged with people for 'Ben Hur' and 'The Ten Commandments', while many other films also attracted large audiences. If a really good film was coming, you had to book a seat. This meant visiting the home of the proprietor, Mr Longhorn, where you were admitted into the hallway and your reservation carefully entered into a posh-looking book. How special you would feel on the night when the letter 'R' was fixed to the back of your seat. It was 1/6 or 1/9 for the rear stalls or the gallery. The latter seats were expensive and out of bounds to us, except for Saturday matinees when children could sit where they liked. Sometimes we would go to the pictures on the first night and spend the second night outside, where we could hear the voices of our favourite stars booming out from the projector room.

As kids, our mischievous antics merited the closest scrutiny by Longhorn himself or, worse, by Doreen the usherette. Watching the film was only a part of our night's entertainment. Anti-social digressions were carried out with ruthless abandon to the annoyance of genuine cinema-goers talking, calling out to friends, facing in the wrong direction and deliberately rustling crisp packets.

We'd blow into empty 'pop' bottles, causing deep sounds to echo throughout the auditorium. Then we'd release the bottles onto the sloping floor, to roll and clank against the metal legs of seats. Sometimes we fired what appeared to be lighted matches into the lights of the projector. Longhorn would stop the film and threaten to throw everyone out. I swear he never realised they were only pieces of paper propelled from elastic bands. There was, of course, the risk of identification, with ejection a likely result. Longhorn's approach however, was easy to detect, for the red glow of his cigarette and balding head (on which the light projecting from the screen reflected) gave away his presence.

Doreen was another matter. She could be secreted in the recess of a fire exit, or even seated surreptitiously on a row. She could tell from fifty seats away just who was doing what. Without moving position, she would chill the blood of the miscreant by screaming 'Stop it!' followed by various threats of retribution. Sometimes, someone in the gallery would walk in front of the projector, causing a gigantic, ghost like shadow to block out whatever drama was unfolding on the screen. This was a reason for feet stamping. For good measure, if the shadow wasn't removed quickly, there would be loud jeers and boos. Yet, despite our misdemeanours, no-one ever got into real trouble. No-one ever damaged anything, not once. Our antics were fairly harmless.

Saturday morning matinee compelled attendance to watch our cowboy heroes Roy Rogers, Gene Autry and Hopalong Cassidy. There was Superman too and, of course, Tarzan. Then there was a serial about Nyoka, the Jungle Girl. I never understood why the same episode was shown every week. Nyoka was trapped in a room as water poured in. When death seemed certain, it ended. Perhaps she died in the next (unseen) episode and old Longhorn hadn't the heart to show it.

Jungle Girl, featuring Nyoka, was a 1941 serial in 15 parts based on a novel by Edgar Rice Burroughs. It was produced by the B movie studio, Republic, whose logo was of an eagle on top of a mountain.

Everyone knew Roy Rogers' four-legged friend was called Trigger, so he was the most popular cowboy of all. For some reason, I always remembered the name of Hopalong Cassidy's horse too. His name was Topper.

As Saturday's matinee finished, an observer at the doors of the Orion would have witnessed a horde of young boys, clad in short trousers, emerge from the building and gallop off in different directions. They'd be shooting at some 'ornery critter' who, though unseen, would be returning fire. Sooner or later they'd dismount for the inevitable shoot-out. It was all good clean fun.

Left: Roy Rogers, known as the 'King of the Cowboys' was the biggest western star in Hollywood from the late 1930s to the early 1950s. His horse, Trigger, became one of the most famous animals in the world.

As we grew up, our attitudes changed. There were no more rolling bottles, no paper missiles. By mid-teens we went to the pictures either because a particularly good film was showing or, equally likely, it was time for another activity – girls. A girl's acceptance of your invitation to the Orion held the promise of a new and exciting adventure. When the lights dimmed it was time to get on with the night's proceedings which, quite likely, was not to watch the film not if you'd managed to book one of the special double seats at the back of the gallery. With the absence of an arm-rest, you could get really close to your partner. Many people must have made their first romantic advances in the almost total darkness of the Orions of this country. It mattered not that there might be a few hundred people present. Everyone else was either riveted to the actions of Errol Flynn or doing the same thing. Yet, when the film ended and the lights came on, everyone broke their loving embraces and nonchalantly looked to the front as though nothing had happened.

In later years, when other cinemas closed, the Orion somehow managed to survive, but then it too shut down its projector. Today, the Orion is still there, but now it's a Bingo Hall with somebody calling out numbers: 'Kelly's Eye' and 'Legs Eleven'. I'd never go there for Bingo. It just wouldn't be the same.

Youngsters fill the seats for a Saturday matinee at the Majestic Cinema in Benwell, Newcastle in 1954. When this cinema was packed the usherette would shout 'two on a seat' and if you look closely I think some of the kids are sharing. There was no health and safety or risk assessments in those days. Do you remember when the film snapped or the projector broke? There would be uproar with booing, stamping of feet and shouts of 'Put a tanner in the gas!'

ABC Minors

A number of cinemas ran clubs for children with 'The ABC Minors' being one of the favourites. They had a song that was sung by the audience with the words on the screen:

We are the boys and girls well known as
Minors of the ABC
And every Saturday all line up
To see the films we like and shout along with glee
We like to laugh and have our sing song
Such a happy crowd are we
We're all pals together
The Minors of the ABC

The Grainger Picture House, Newcastle around 1930. The Grainger was best known for showing the same films week after week if they were popular. You often saw adverts in local newspapers saying 'held over for another week'. Many people have told me that they remember seeing 'The Quiet Man' here in the 1950s. It is the story of a retired boxer, played by John Wayne, who retires to Ireland for a 'quiet life' then falls in love with Maureen O'Hara and has an epic fight with Victor McLaglen.

PICTUREDROME
TRIMDON GRANGE

Week Commencing Monday, 31st January

Mon. Continuous from 6 p.m.　Tues. to Fri. Once Nightly 6-45
Sat. 2 Houses 6 & 8-30　Sun. at 8.　Prices: 6d., 7d., 1/-, 1/6

MONDAY and TUESDAY　　　　　FOR TWO DAYS
Gary Cooper : Barry Jones
RETURN TO PARADISE
(IN TECHNICOLOR)

WEDNESDAY and THURSDAY　　　FOR TWO DAYS
Clark Gable : John Hodiak
ACROSS THE WIDE MISSOURI
(IN TECHNICOLOR)

FRIDAY and SATURDAY　　　　　FOR TWO DAYS
Charles Vanel : Peter Van Eyck
THE WAGES OF FEAR

Sunday,　　　　Walter Pidgeon, Peter Lawford
The Red Danube

John Wayne fights Victor McLaglen in the classic 'The Quiet Man'. The film was directed by John Ford who was better known for his many westerns – often with John Wayne – that were much loved by North East audiences in the years either side of the Second World War. Some local cinemas were known as 'The Ranch' because they showed so many of these westerns.

Left: Most communities had at least one cinema and here is an advert from the 1950s for the Picturedrome, Trimdon Grange. The programme changed four times a week. On Friday and Saturday they were showing the French film 'The Wages of Fear' – the gripping story of lorry drivers transporting explosives through a jungle in South America and the first film with subtitles to have a major release in Britain.

Let's Face the Music and Dance

Right: The Oxford Galleries in Newcastle. For many years the Oxford was one of the most popular venues in the North East and, whenever I talk to someone about dance halls, it is one of the first to be mentioned. Up until the 1950s there were dozens of dance halls in the North East as well as dances held at church halls, miners' institutes or Co-op halls. Even some of these smaller venues had sprung floors that made dancing easier on the feet.

Local author, Jim Harland, remembers the Roxy Ballroom in Blyth:

'The Roxy was tremendously popular particularly for teenagers on a Saturday afternoon. It was there you not only met the girls but were also taught how to dance properly. Tuition was given by a ballroom dancer called George Pitkeathley and his wife and partner Betty who took us through all forms of dance. Even now I can still perform Latin American, Old Time and Modern but am a bit rusty on American square dancing.

'From the Saturday afternoon sessions you graduated to the evening sessions with Modern dancing on a Monday and Saturday, Old Time on a Tuesday, private functions on Wednesday, Barn, Scottish and American square dancing on Thursday and a mixed programme on Friday.

'Tommy Bell and his ten-piece orchestra provided music at the Roxy for many years. Tommy was regarded as the 'Mr Music' of the town and his musicians were always impeccably dressed in evening suits and bow ties. Tommy, an excellent accordionist, was a bit of a character who, on occasions, was not beyond halting a dance in mid-stream to berate the dancers for not doing it properly.'

Left: Tommy Bell and his orchestra at the Roxy Ballroom in Blyth.

Rock Around The Clock

The age of the dance halls and the big bands started to come to an end in the mid 1950s when 'Rock and Roll' was born. One of the earliest stars of this era was Bill Haley whose song 'Rock Around The Clock' was a massive hit and the title of a film that took cinemas by storm. Some picture houses allowed people to dance in the aisles, and in front of the screen, and several in the North East did this. I spoke to one lady who saw 'Rock Around The Clock' in an old flea pit with her friends who all danced along. What they did not realise in the darkness was that all of this dancing had lifted the muck and dust that had been in this cinema for years. When the lights came on at the end, they saw how filthy their faces and clothes were.

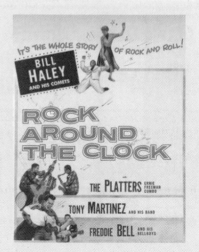

Pupils from Silksworth Modern School dancing at their Christmas party in the 1950s. For today's youngsters one of the highlights of their time at school is the prom – a celebration of graduation. The finest dresses and suits are worn and some arrive in style in limos or even vintage cars.

DANCING made EASY!

BE POPULAR, LEARN AT HOME WITH
MOVING PICTURES

Learning to dance by the Movie Method is fun, and so simple—just pictures to follow in the privacy of your own home. No need now to memorise long technical descriptions, you copy the movements of two first-class demonstrators. Movement in slow-motion by the unique Cine-Tutor Movie Books makes it possible to become a good dancer and popular partner quicker and easier than ever before. No apparatus required. Hundreds have learned by the easy Movie Method—SO CAN YOU—Surprise and amaze your friends, don't be a " sitter-out " any longer.

Over 1,500 PICTURES: 20 MOVIE SEQUENCES:

Send 2½d. stamp to-day to:
MOVIE METHOD
Studio 145
9 Cursitor Street
London, E.C.4

WRITE TODAY! for FREE LITERATURE and DETAILS

EASY TO FOLLOW ACTION

Above you see one of the famous Cine-Tutor Movie Books, which give you life-like movement in slow motion—a miniature movie in your own hand.

I enclose 2½d. stamp. Please send full details of the Movie Method.

....

....

....

B145...

If you did not take dance lessons you could learn using the 'Movie Method'. This was a series of books that you flicked the pages and the still photos gave the dance movements that you would follow. It claimed you could easily learn to dance this way and that you could: 'Surprise and amaze your friends, don't be a "sitter-out" any longer.'

An advert from the Northumberland Gazette for local dances seeing in the New Year of 1951. At Wooler were Johnny Dryburgh's Revellers who: 'will make you crack your heels.'

Going to the Match

A goal is scored by Newcastle United at St James' Park in the 1950s. The stadium looks very different from today. Most of the supporters are standing with no all-seater stadiums in those days. A few young lads are sitting around the pitch and in the straw used to protect the grass in winter. You would be arrested and banned from the ground if you got onto the pitch these days. There is also no roof over the heads of the fans and no replica shirts that almost everyone wears now. One lone policeman watches the action with no stewards and their hi-viz jackets.

A massive queue outside St James' Park for tickets for an FA Cup tie in 1955.

Right: A group of Sunderland players training at Roker Park after the Second World War. You get a good view of the terraces behind them – again no roof. These players were not paid the extravagant wages of modern players but they were still idolised by the fans. Up until 1961 a maximum wage was in force and even the top stars of the day were paid only £20 a week.

The most famous player of the post-war era was Stanley Matthews. It was said that he would add an extra 10,000 spectators onto the attendance whenever he played away from home. My Nana wasn't a football fan but she wanted to see Stanley Matthews when he came to Roker Park and Granda took her to the match. But, being a small woman, she couldn't see the players from where they were stood on the terraces so Granda picked her up, she saw Matthews and, when he put her down, Nana said, 'We're going home now!'

Left: An advert for Stanley Matthews Football Boots from Co-operative Stores. Matthews was one of the first footballers to sign a sponsorship deal and he would often make personal appearances at Co-op Stores on the morning of an away match.

Right: It was not only Newcastle and Sunderland that were popular and matches between local sides drew great crowds – and celebrities. Here, Eddie Calvert – 'The Man With The Golden Trumpet' – kicks off a match between Easington Lane FC and Eyemouth.

Beside the Seaside

A packed Redcar beach in the late 1950s. There are rows and rows of tents, all full of families packed together, having travelled by bus from all around the area. People hired the tents for the day and inside you would change into your bathing costume so you could swim in the sea. Others had a windbreak as a protection from the elements and how many of you remember struggling to put on your swimwear and holding a towel around you at the same time (not easy). In the background you can see the rolling waves of the North Sea and, in the foreground, one of the favourite rides – the Shuggy Boats.

How many remember wearing a lovely 'knitted swimsuit' made by your mother or even your grandmother? Remember the feeling when you first went into the sea? 'Oh my goodness' that costume felt like you were in a sack of potatoes with the amount of water it could hold. And how it stretched so the same swimsuit that was made to fit when you were two years old would still be around when you were five.

An advert for Roker and Seaburn – the holiday resort 'on your doorstep'. Local resorts went into decline as cheap package holidays abroad became popular from the 1960s.

Peter Newton, of Ferryhill, on the beach wearing his knitted swimming costume in July 1949.

Rough Sea, Tynemouth Bathing Pool. 6845

A postcard view of Tynemouth Bathing Pool. This photograph has been taken on a stormy day but, during the summertime and Bank Holidays, Tynemouth Long Sands would be packed with visitors. Most would just come for the day and take with them everything they needed. Food would be a plate pie or seaside sandwiches, normally egg and tomato ... and sand! You would take your own teapot and make tea on the beach by getting a jug of hot water from a nearby kiosk. All the family would go but it was normally the mams who looked after the kids while the dads waited for the pub or club to open. The men didn't have beachwear and would be dressed in their suits. Perhaps they would wear a knotted handkerchief and then roll up a trouser leg to go plodgin'.

Trips would sometimes be organised by the Sunday schools or the workingmen's club. A day trip to the seaside may have been the only holiday for some. In a care home in Gateshead I once spoke to a gentleman who went on a poor bairns' trip in the 1930s. He said a group of children were taken to Amble and the highlight of the day was when they got their food. Their lunch was a pie but, when you were given it, your hand was stamped so you couldn't have another one. This gentlemen could remember it clearly and he told me how he and his friends hid round a corner while they ate their pies. They then rubbed off the mark on their hands so they could go back and claim another one. Often when I am in Gateshead and I start to tell the story of the poor bairns' trip, someone will say 'You got your hand stamped!'

TRIP. 1923. R.O. WILSON CONSETT.

Right: Dozens of buses for the Poor Bairns' trip from Consett to Whitley Bay in 1923.

SPANISH CITY WHITLEY BAY.

SPANISH CITY (IN GROUNDS) WHITLEY BAY.

Above and right: Two postcards of the famous Spanish City and grounds, Whitley Bay. One lady in Winlaton, near Gateshead, told me that when she was younger her family could afford a few nights in a guest house in Whitley Bay. This was just after the Second World War and in those days it was very rare to go away for more than a day trip. When the taxi arrived in their street to take them to the train station for the start of their journey, half the street came out to wave them off as if they were going on a long journey!

School Camp, Blackhall Rocks 13600

Left: A postcard of School Camp, Blackhall Rocks, County Durham. You were lucky if you had a holiday before the Second World War so a trip to a camp such as this would be a great adventure for a youngster. The card was posted to Windermere Street, Gateshead in 1937. The message reads: 'I am enjoying myself immensely down here … I hope you are in the pink again.'

Above: Families enjoying a stay in the chalets at Crimdon Dene, County Durham. Other seaside destinations for day trips and holidays included: Cullercoats, Newbiggin, Cresswell, South Shields and Marsden Bay.

Right: An advert for Mr Whippy ice cream – always a seaside favourite!

By the early 1950s families started to travel further afield and for many a holiday would be a trip to Butlins.

Above: The indoor and outdoor swimming pools at Butlins holiday camp, Filey.

Right: The dining hall at Filey's Butlins camp. The well dressed staff are preparing the tables for hundreds of guests.

Tatie Picking

by Mary Foster Taylor

I was twelve years old when I had the idea to go tatie picking. Why not, all my Lynemouth School pals were going; it was the chance to earn a little pocket money in the Blackberry Week October holiday. My dad said no, he thought I was too young and girls should not be taking that sort of a job. My brother Tom saved the day. I approached him and he persuaded Dad to let me go. On the first day all the village youngsters were picked up by tractor and trailer at 7.30 am and taken to the Long Field at Ellington. Names were called out by the farm steward, Geordie Thompson, and the name Tom Foster came up time and time again but no one responded. Finally I was the only child left and Geordie asked my name. When I replied Mary Foster, he said, 'Oh right you must be Tom Foster's sister.' He then paced out the picking plots at ten-yard intervals and I took my place in the potato chain.

Mary Foster.

It was hard work picking the big chipper taties the tractor unearthed and some of the lads tried to cheat by moving their markers and reducing the size of the plot to be worked. At break-time farmhands would travel round the field with a huge tea urn on the back of a tractor trailer supplying drinks which were well received by the thirsty pickers. Each night, just before we were taken home at 4 pm, every child was allowed a pail of potatoes for home use and often we took a snaggie (turnip) from the next field. Often on the trailer ride home we would pass a trailer load of pickers from Boghall or Blakemoor farms and a free-for-all tatie fight erupted. Taties could be found all over the roads and paths, much to the joy of the local villagers who would gather up and use the flying taties.

Potato picking at Barlow Fell near High Spen in 1964. It certainly looks like back-breaking work.

Friday was pay day and boy was I pleased as my back and legs were stiff and sore with the continuous bending. All the children were lined up and Geordie handed each one their dues in a brown packet, 10 shillings for the boys (50p) and 7/6 for the girls (37½p) for a week's work. When I received mine it was marked Tom Foster and inside I had the boy's wage. To this day I still do not know whether Geordie had forgotten to change the name or if being friends with my brother had been a factor in me being the best paid girl tatie picker in the village.

Above: Sunderland lads on their way home after tatie picking at Cleadon in the 1950s.

Turnips ... Snaggies ... Snammys ... Snadgers

In Mary's story she says that turnips in Ellington were called snaggies. As I've went round the North East, I've heard the turnip being called a snammy, baggie, tuggie or snadger. I grew up in Sunderland and on Halloween us kids would put a candle in a turnip that we called a narkie (today the kids use a pumpkin!). I think it's strange that an ordinary vegetable such as a turnip has all of these different names around the region.

Right: At Hedley West Farm, near Stanley in the 1950s are farmer's daughter, Josie Swinburne and her friend Marion Ross.

In the Bleak Midwinter

Before the days of central heating do you remember those freezing cold nights? Perhaps waking up to frost on the inside of the windows! A hot water bottle such as the one on the right was a much needed bed warmer. It was normally filled with water but I have spoken to some people who would fill the bottle with sand and then put it into the oven to heat up. One lady told me that her mother filled the bottle with salt as she thought that was the best to retain the heat. If you couldn't afford one of these, an old ginger beer bottle would do; or a hot brick or oven shelf wrapped in a towel.

Left: Men clearing snow in Belford, Northumberland during the Second World War.

In the winter of 1940/41 the temperature dropped to ten degrees below freezing in parts of the North East on the night of the 20th January. In February 1941 snow fell continually for three days. All this terrible weather and the war was on!

Six years later, in 1947, some areas of the North East had a covering of snow from late January to mid March. February saw some of the lowest average daily temperatures recorded in the century. In the years after the war there was also fuel rationing and power cuts at this time.

Right: Another bad winter was in 1963 and here is the Tyne Bridge and Swing Bridge over a frozen River Tyne. The bad weather started that year on the 2nd January with a three day blizzard. The icy weather continued until the thaw finally came in March.

Christmas

Christmas used to be a much simpler time than today. There would be none of the extravagant gifts youngsters have now with perhaps a homemade toy being your main present years ago. Nuts, fruit, small toys (stocking fillers) and a shiny 'new' penny would be found in your stocking – an old coin polished by your dad on Christmas Eve.

Right: Annuals were popular gifts at Christmas and here is the 'School Friend' from 1956.

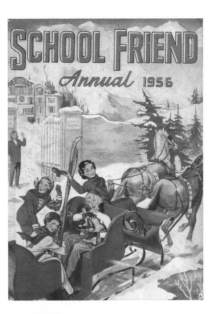

An advert for the toys at Blacketts in Sunderland from 1955 with cowboy outfits, space suits, trikes and prams. Also advertised is the chance to see Santa (*left*).

Christmas Dinner

What did you have for Christmas dinner? For many years it wasn't turkey which only became fashionable from the 1960s. For many years chicken for Christmas was more common or sometimes a goose with the mams using the grease from the bird to rub on your chest for colds.

Right: A lady picks out the turkey she would like for Christmas from her well-stocked local butcher.

Christmas Cake and Stocking Fillers

by Dorothy A. Rand

The earliest preparations in our house were making the Christmas puddings and cake. The puddings were made to a wartime recipe which resulted in a lighter, less rich pudding. Mam liked this so much she used this recipe for another forty years! It included breadcrumbs made by baking slices of bread in the oven and then crushing them with a rolling pin. Another ingredient was grated carrot. The smell of the cake baking in the oven was wonderful. I loved to watch Mam decorating the cake, she made marzipan from ground almonds and egg yolks. Any trimmings left over became my property. I used dates and walnuts to make sweets. I was also allowed to decorate biscuits with leftover white icing, using the icing tube to pipe 'stars'.

It was easy for me to be excited about Christmas but it meant extra work for my mother. Christmas preparations did not start so early then, presents were bought locally or made at home. One year – 1949 or 1950 – my mother sent for a Samuel Drivers catalogue and ordered several items, including a bottle of Egg Flip. I don't to this day know what is in Egg Flip. My parents were Sons of Temperance and strict teetotallers. Our cat took one whiff of it, I can still see her, in front of the coal scuttle, lapping Egg Flip from her saucer.

We didn't put our decorations up until maybe the day before Christmas Eve. Dad particularly loved the decorations and all the festivity of Christmas, possibly because he'd been born on Christmas Eve in 1905. Grandma said he'd spoilt her Christmas dinner that year! He liked as much as possible draped around the living room, there were no Christmas lights for us, they came soon after 1950.

My grandparents' Christmas decorations, mostly bought in the 1890s, were sent for me. They were, and still are in a wooden box from a shop, used to deliver blacking from the manufacturer. The main decorations are a large bronze-coloured heavy glass

A family tradition was to keep the Christmas cake until cutting it at midnight on New Year's Eve. The Christmas cake is on the table and Ena Noble can be seen pouring ginger wine watched by daughter Dorothy.

bauble and a bright pink swan decorated with a blue-robed Santa. There were many others plus lovely red and green chenille wall drapes trimmed with silver bells.

Before Christmas Day all tradesmen who called at the house had to be caught and given their 'Christmas box', about two shillings at this time. The same people were also invited in for cake and wine on their first visit after New Year.

The food on Christmas Day was entirely different to the rest of the year. Chicken was then a luxury to be had once a year, for Christmas. Mam worried about chickens. The giblets were immediately discarded then she washed the carcass thoroughly inside and out, pulling out any loose bits from the cavity. She did not stuff the chicken, but cooked the stuffing separately. She made it from chopped boiled onions, white breadcrumbs and sage crumbled from a bunch of dried sage bought at the Co-op greengrocers. I looked forward in due course, to being given the wishbone.

With the chicken and stuffing we had potatoes, sprouts and turnip, followed by Christmas pudding and white sauce. After all of this we didn't want much tea. We had the blackberry tart, the Christmas cake was not to be cut into until New Year. We were, like the chicken, well roasted at Christmas, in the small room the table was very near the oven, and Dad had kept very large pieces of coal to one side for Christmas.

I was never disappointed with my presents, I always had the main present of my choice and many others besides. My parents were not well off but they took a great deal of time and trouble over my presents. I realised that I had much more than them; the highlight of my Dad's childhood Christmas had been a cheap tin toy, soon broken and my Mam's was a bar of chocolate and a sugar mouse. My presents were kept in a large wicker laundry basket, behind the rarely-used front door and brought out to display to visitors whom I'd try to inveigle into playing some of the games with me – maybe Snap or Happy Families, Snakes and Ladders, Ludo or Dominoes. There was no TV then to distract, the focus was on people.

Everything was done according to tradition, without deviation. My toys were dispersed from the laundry basket and Dad, who loved the decorations, was sad to see them come down on Twelfth Night to be packed away in their large wicker hamper.

I went to bed early on Christmas Eve to make Christmas Day come sooner. I left a stocking on the bottom of the bed. On Christmas morning, as every other morning. I wasn't allowed to go downstairs until the fire was lit, the room was warmed up and breakfast was ready. But I had my stocking! This was a new navy blue wool long pit stocking of Dad's, all tantalising lumps and bumps. The further down the stocking your hand went to fish out the presents, the more the stocking clung to your arm. Several 'stocking-fillers' were in my stocking, maybe a novelty soap in a box, bath salts, a kaleidoscope, a tin of toffees or new crayons. At the bottom there was always a tangerine, an apple and some nuts. A bag of mixed nuts was bought once a year –

Dorothy with her doll's pram (homemade), 1949.

Brazils, almonds, hazelnuts and walnuts. Carefully cracked walnut shells provided cradles for tiny dolls. My main present was always discovered when I went downstairs. For some years after the war these were always made at home by my parents and Cousin Stan, Dad's bachelor nephew, who was a painter and decorator, good at making things and very artistic. Dad was a colliery joiner, so woodwork was his province, Mam was artistic and a good needlewoman.

I love things which kept me busy – paints, crayons, activity books, colouring books and 'magic' painting books which only needed plain water to reveal the different colours. I had sewing cards, a knitting set, a baking set, plasticine, a hot water bottle like a panda and some bright pink slippers. I was obsessed with stationary from an early age (and still am) and received children's writing sets, post office sets, pens, pencils and rubbers. I also had lots of books. Unfortunately, my mother's stepmother did not understand little girls – my cousin and myself were regular recipients of dark blue or green interlock school knickers from the Co-op!

Dorothy Rand in the spectacular winter of 1947. Not only is she holding a Christmas present but she is also wearing some as well.

New Year

After Christmas it was on to less hectic preparations for New Year. Before midnight mats were shaken, the ashes taken out, and then it was time to go to the back door to listen to the bells of the church ring in the New Year. Cousin Stan, being dark-haired, was first foot, bearing a piece of coal for good luck. Then there was ginger wine and Christmas cake and it was time for bed. My family started the year secure in the knowledge that all bills, even very small ones had been paid. They wanted to start the New Year on the basis of not owing any money (except their mortgage).

Childhood Games

How did youngsters spend their free time in the days before computers, video games and television? Imagination was the key before all those gadgets were invented and games were played with your friends in the fresh air. For the boys it would be football, cricket, marbles or mount-a-kitty while the girls would play two-baller, skips and hop scotch (sometimes called bays or itchy-dabbers). Everyone took part in games like cannon (with a can and sticks); tiggy (shouting skinch when you wanted a break); diablos; chucks; tops and whips.

Do you remember even playing knocky-nine-doors – it would be called anti-social behaviour today!

Left: Hula hoops are not easy and here are some mixed results from the Shildon Scouts Carnival in 1959. They were first introduced in 1957 and within a few years over 100 million had been sold.

'Boolers' were popular toys for many years. The hoops made of metal or wood were 'booled' along the street with your hand, a stick or special metal rod. There are records of children playing with this toy as long ago as the 15th century and in Victorian times the game was seen as a nuisance.

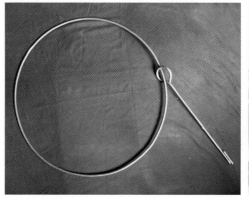

Above: One of the young lads in the photograph from the early 1900s is holding a booler.

Left: Andrew Clark, the author of this book, shows his skill with a booler in the schoolyard at Beamish Museum. The ones at Beamish have the hoop and the stick connected whereas most would have been separate.

One gentleman who lived in Byker recalled taking part in a booler race around Brough Park in Newcastle in the 1940s. He said dozens of kids took part on a track that is normally used for greyhounds or speedway.

A perfect 'action photograph' showing the game of 'Mount-a-kitty' in Ashington in the 1950s. Also called 'Mount-a-cuddy' or 'Mont-a-kitty', one person would have his back to a wall while others bent down in a line in front of him. Then one-by-one you would run and jump on their back. This was a rough game with the lads on top hoping to collapse the line while those bending down trying to throw off the ones on their back.

Right: A crowd of lads watch this game. While playing they would shout: 'Mount-a-kitty, Mount-a-kitty, one, two, three ... fall off, fall off, fall of me!'

You would be a lucky lad if you had a football like this one – a caser or casie. Made of leather, it was great when it was dry but got very heavy when it rained as the ball soaked up water. Those laces could be deadly if you headed it. It is a very different football from today's lightweight, plastic ones.

A great pair of old football boots. The kit was much more basic and there were no coloured boots like you see now.

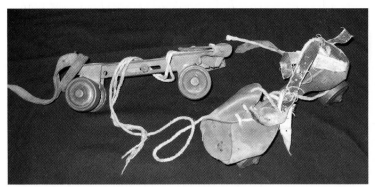

Roller skating was very popular in the 1930s, 40s and 50s and it helped that it was easier to skate on roads with a lot fewer cars. With less traffic you were also free to ride your bogie made of a few pieces of wood and old pram wheels or in winter it was the turn of homemade sledges.

Top right: Two girls in a back lane of the colliery village of Silksworth around 1930. One of them has the remains of a pram. I wonder if those wheels were later used on a bogie.

Skips

Here are a few skipping rhymes:

All in together girls,
Never mind the weather girls,
I saw Esau
Sitting on the sea-saw

The wind, the wind, the wind blows higher,
In comes (you say their name) from the sky.
Isn't she beautiful?
Isn't she sweet?
Tell me the boy, she'd like to meet!

(Then you would go through all of the boys' names to embarrass her)

All the boys in high school aren't very nice,
Except for (a boy's name) he's alright.
He took me to the pictures and sat me on his knee,
And said (her name) will you marry me.
Yes … no … maybe so … Yes … no … maybe so …

(If you stop skipping on yes you would have to marry him)

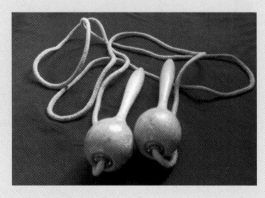

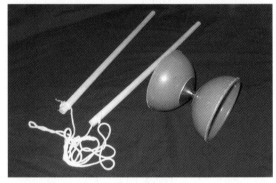

You needed plenty of practise to be good at diablos.

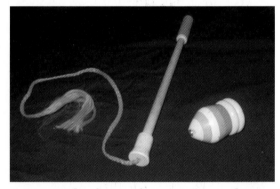

A top and whip – do you remember colouring the top with chalk to make a pattern when it was spinning?

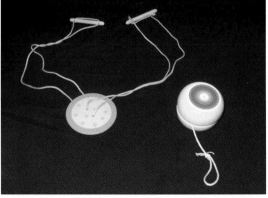

On the right a yo-yo and on the left what some people call a 'whizzer' – a disc spun round with string.

It Never Seemed to Rain

by Jack Curtis

The seasons of the year were marked with various phases: tops and whips would have a run, hitchy quoit for girls, skates next, diablos, crackers, kick the tin and skipping ropes which would bring our mothers out and communal skipping would be the order of the day, with everyone joining in. Even our mothers would recapture their youth and in they would go with their pinafores held in their hand, with whoops and laughter. They were great times, great people, lovely days.

We made slides across the school yard when it froze and would queue up to take turns to run up then slide across the yard.

Other times we would play knocky-out with white pot tossies, spending the whole playtime at this game, ending up with bulging pockets if you had your eye in. Cricket was also played in the yard during the summer when our headmaster would invariably join in to show his skills off to us lads. At other times we were taken by bus and then tram to play football on some local pitches.

Those were halcyon days when it never seemed to rain.

Jack Curtis with his pals drinking milk at Moor Board School Infants, Sunderland in 1935. Left to right: Conrad Culkin, Jack, Bernie McCue, Fred Lincoln, Jimmy Urch and Billy Corner. They even had flowers on the table.

Left: A back lane cricket match. Note the wicket which has the stumps on a stand that allowed you to play with them in the street or schoolyard. If kit like this wasn't available, a wicket was chalked on a wall or a dustbin was used.

More fun and games with lads having a wheel barrow race in the 1930s.

A boys versus girls game of rounders in the late 1950s.

Also available from Summerhill Books

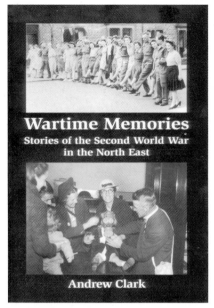

Wartime Memories
Stories of the Second World War in the North East

Andrew Clark

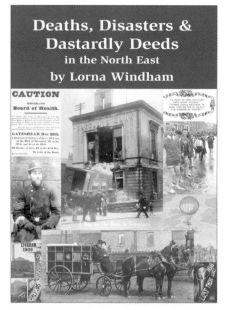

Deaths, Disasters & Dastardly Deeds
in the North East
by Lorna Windham

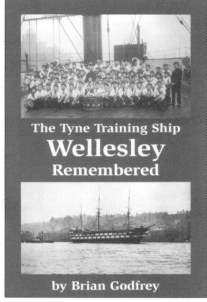

The Tyne Training Ship
Wellesley Remembered

by Brian Godfrey

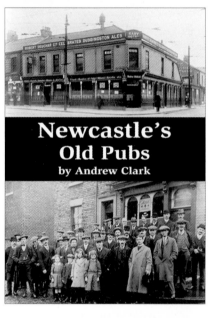

Newcastle's Old Pubs
by Andrew Clark

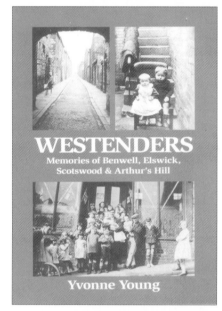

WESTENDERS
Memories of Benwell, Elswick, Scotswood & Arthur's Hill

Yvonne Young

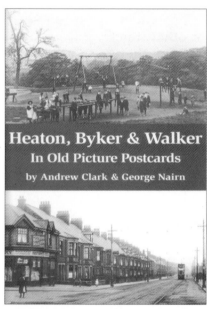

Heaton, Byker & Walker
In Old Picture Postcards
by Andrew Clark & George Nairn

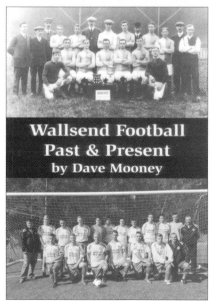

Wallsend Football Past & Present
by Dave Mooney

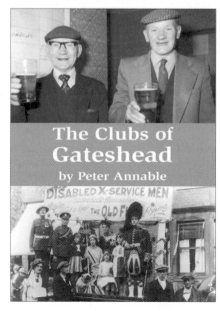

The Clubs of Gateshead
by Peter Annable

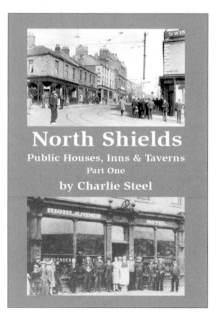

North Shields
Public Houses, Inns & Taverns
Part One
by Charlie Steel